Knitting Basics for Beginners

Step By Step Visual Guide – Learn to Knit Like a Pro in Less than a Week!

By

Katrina Gale

D1492870

CSB Academy Publishing Co.
P. O. Box 966
Semmes, Alabama 36575, USA

Cover Design & Illustration

By

Jane Keller

First Edition

TABLE OF CONTENTS

INTRODUCTION

You have picked up this book because you are a smart and creative person and you want to learn how to knit. That's wonderful! I am happy to introduce you to knitting. Before we get started, I just want to remind you that you will be learning a new mechanical skill. This means your fingers will feel awkward holding the needles and manipulating the yarn for the first little while. It doesn't take long before your body begins to memorize the movements and your knitting will pick up speed and begin to look smoother and more professional.

However, for the first little while try to be patient, concentrate on the required movement of the needles and yarn and find the most comfortable way for YOU to knit.

You are going to make errors. This a good thing because we learn more from our mistakes than we do from performing a task perfectly. In Chapter 7 I will discuss the most common problems beginners run into and various ways to solve them. You always have options in knitting.

We will begin with simple squares or swatches of knitting because they knit up quickly and you can use them to compare examples of different types of stitches, increases, and decreases to see what they might look like in a completed garment. You can make notes about what you have learned and attach them to the swatches with a safety-pin, so you have a resource you can go back to anytime you need to refresh your memory.

Ready to get started?

CHAPTER 1 - EQUIPMENT

To begin you need nothing more than a ball of yarn and a pair of needles. Later on, you will also need a measuring tape or ruler, a couple of straight pins, and a medium-sized crochet hook for fixing mistakes.

There is no need to spend a lot of money on your practice equipment. I would suggest using an inexpensive, smooth, medium-weight yarn in a light color. At some point, you are going to have to count your stitches, and you do not want to strain your eyes trying to count stitches in navy or black wool.

You can find the weight of the yarn on the yarn label. Most yarns today have a standard numbering system. A medium yarn is a number 4 yarn, which is also known as worsted or afghan yarn. If you are not sure, just ask another knitter or one of the salespeople in your local yarn shop. (See the Chart)

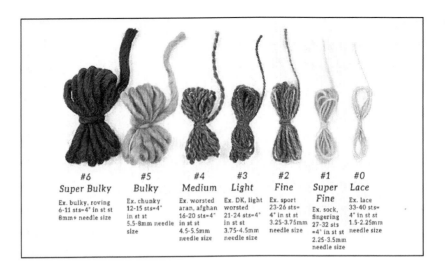

#6	#5	#4	#3	#2	#1	#0
Super Bulky	Bulky	Medium	Light	Fine	Super Fine	Lace
Ex. bulky, roving 6-11 sts=4" in st st 8mm+ needle size	Ex. chunky 12-15 sts=4" in st st 5.5-8mm needle size	Ex. worsted aran, afghan 16-20 sts=4" in st st 4.5-5.5mm needle size	Ex. DK, light worsted 21-24 sts=4" in st st 3.75-4.5mm needle size	Ex. sport 23-26 sts= 4" in st st 3.25-3.75mm needle size	Ex. sock, fingering 27-32 sts =4" in st st 2.25-3.5mm needle size	Ex. lace 33-40 sts= 4" in st st 1.5-2.25mm needle size

Today knitting needles are made from many materials including plastic, metal, bamboo, and wood. You may need to try a few different types of needles before you settle on a particular type that works well for you. I have found that plastic needles can be sticky, keeping the yarn from moving from the left needle to the right needle smoothly. Metal needles can be too slippery, depending on the softness of the yarn you are using, and your stitches can accidentally slip off.

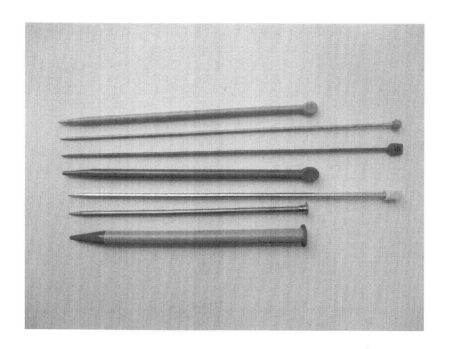

Knitting needles are relatively inexpensive to purchase, and you can always borrow a pair from a fellow knitter to try the different materials before you make your final purchase. I would recommend a US size 6 knitting needle (this is a size 4 mm using the metric system). See the char below.

KNITTING NEEDLE CONVERSION CHART		
IMPERIAL	METRIC	US
14	2	0
13	2.25	1
12	2.5	...
12	2.75	2
11	3	3
10	3.25	3
9	3.5	4
9	3.75	5
8	4	6
7	4.5	7
6	5	8
5	5.5	9
4	6	10
3	6.5	10.5
2	7	...
1	7.5	...
0	8	11
00	9	13
000	10	15

You've got your yarn, you've got your needles, you're all set. Let's get started!

CHAPTER 2 - CASTING ON

Casting on creates the first row of stitches. There are over 50 methods of casting on, but for beginners, the easiest and most elastic cast on method is the thumb method (also known as the *e-cast on*). The thumb method is used when a very elastic edge is needed, or when the rows immediately following it will be knit in garter stitch or stockinette stitch.

Tail and Yarn

The *tail* is the thread at the beginning or end of a ball of yarn that is not knit but left hanging, to be sewn in later. The *yarn* is the rest of the ball and is what you knit with, this is also often called the *working yarn*.

The thumb cast on begins with a slip knot, which creates your first stitch. To create a slip knot:

1) Wind the yarn around two fingers twice. Place the yarn on the back, behind the loops over your fingers.

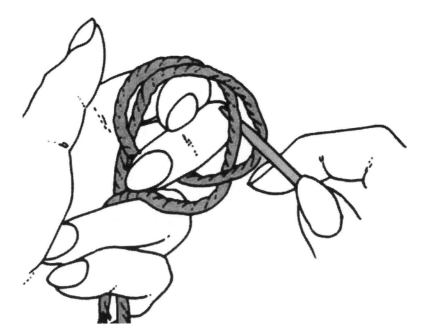

Fig. 1

2) Using a knitting needle pull the back thread through the front one to form a loop around the needle.

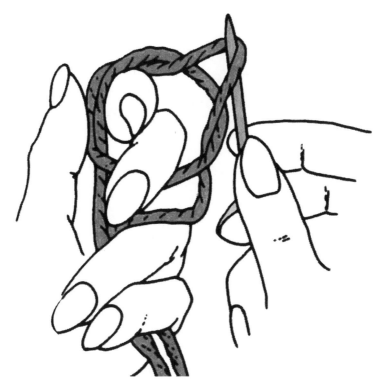

Fig. 2

3) Pull on the tail or the yarn, or both together, to tighten
the loop around the needle.

Fig. 3

The Thumb Cast On

1) Measure out approximately three feet of yarn from the tail of your ball and make a slip knot in your yarn at that point.

2) Place the slip knot on one of your knitting needles and pull on the yarn tail to snug the stitch up against the needle. Do not make it too tight, you will need a little room to insert your other needle into the slip knot.

3) Hold the needle in your right hand with the ball end of the yarn over your first finger. Wind the loose end of the yarn around your left thumb from front to back.

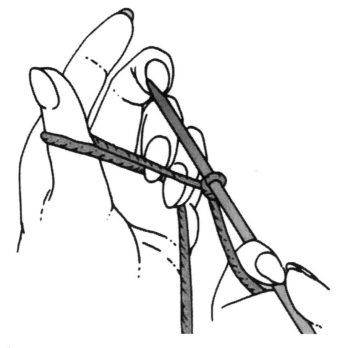

Fig. 4.

4) Insert the needle through the yarn on your thumb.

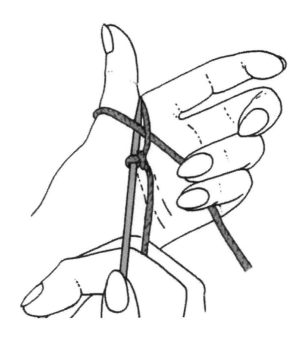

Fig. 5

5) With your right forefinger, take the yarn over the point
   of the needle.

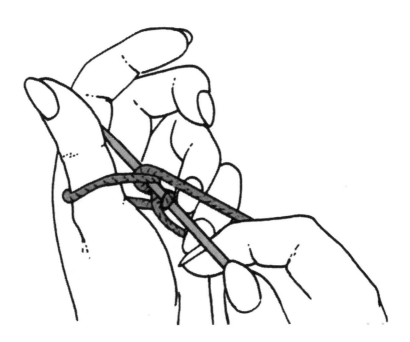

Fig. 6

6) Pull the loop through to form the first stitch.

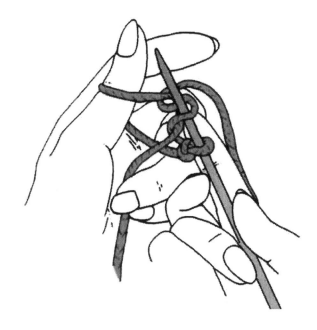

Fig. 7

7) Remove your thumb from the yarn and pull the loose end to tighten and secure the stitch.

Fig. 8

Repeat from 3 through 7 until the required number of stitches are cast on.

It's time for you to give it a try. Make a slip knot and cast on 15 stitches. Want to try it again? Gently hold the stitches with your left hand and with your right hand pull the needle out of the stitches. Check your slip knot, if it hasn't come undone place it back on the needle and cast on again. If the slip knot has come undone, simply make a new slip knot and try casting on again. It will get easier each time you try.

As you practice your thumb method cast on try to get your tension as smooth as possible. You must snug the yarn up to needle, but not too tight so that the stitches are difficult to put your needle through them. If you do not pull tightly enough, you will end up with loops in your cast on that will hang from the bottom of your knitting. Remember practice makes perfect.

Have you practiced a few times? You are now ready to knit your first 15 stitches.

Making the Knit Stitch

A knit stitch is simply a loop of yarn on your knitting needle. The knit stitch is formed by taking the working yarn around the right-hand needle and drawing it through a stitch on the left-hand needle, as we will show below. To form the knit stitch, I suggest you use your right hand to carry the working yarn. Don't worry if you feel awkward or slow, you will soon adjust.

1) With 15 stitches cast on and with the yarn held behind the needles, away from your body, put the right-hand needle, from front to back, through the first stitch on the left-hand needle so that the right-hand needle sits behind the left-hand needle.

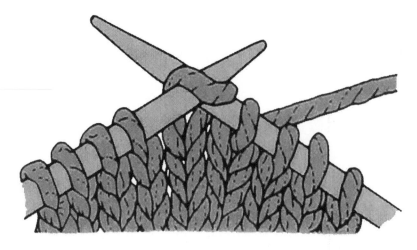

Fig. 9

2) Holding both needles with your left-hand close to where they cross, wind the yarn around the right-hand needle with your right hand.

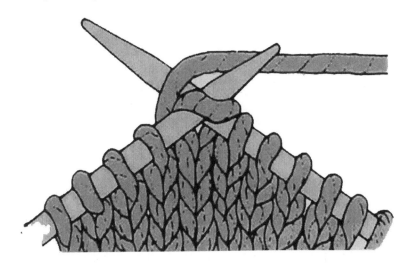

Fig. 10

3) This will create a loop on the right-hand needle. Pull the loop through using your right-hand needle.

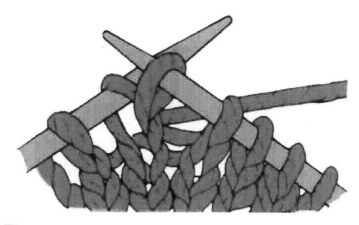

Fig. 11

4) Slip the original stitch you first entered off the left-hand
   needle. One knit stitch completed.

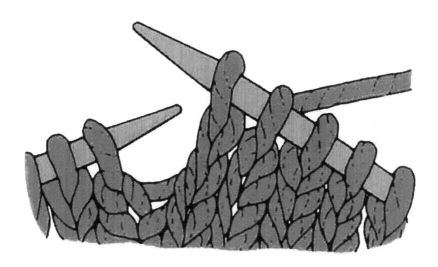

Fig. 12

Repeat these four steps until all the stitches on the left-
hand needle have been knitted over to the right-hand

needle. You have completed one row of knitting. Congratulations!

To continue you simply switch the needles to the opposite hands. Put the empty needle in your right hand and the needle with all of the stitches on it in your left hand.

Holding the working yarn in your right hand begin at number 1 above and continue knitting across the row.

CHAPTER 3 - HOLDING THE NEEDLES AND MANAGING THE YARN

Most knitters carry the yarn in their right hand, with the yarn threaded through their fingers to provide a certain amount of tension. There are a variety of ways to hold the yarn, and the only right way is the way that is the most comfortable for YOU. I will describe the most common method below, so you have somewhere to start, but there is no one right way to hold the yarn, what matters is that your hands are comfortable. Knitting should be an enjoyable activity and should not cause repetitive strain injuries. Experiment until you find what works for you.

Holding the Needles

The right-hand needle is held as if you were holding a pencil. As you cast on and work the first one or two rows the needle is held this way. As the work becomes longer let the thumb slide under the knitting, grasping the needle from below.

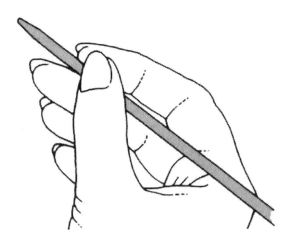

Fig. 13

The left-hand needle is held lightly over its top. The thumb and forefinger are used to control the tip of the needle.

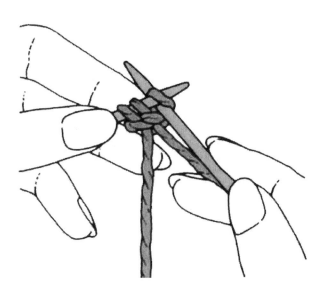

Fig. 14

Holding the Yarn - Method One

Holding the yarn in the right hand, pass the yarn under your little finger, then around the same finger, this gives the yarn some tension, then over your third finger, under the center finger, and over your index finger. You will use your index finger to pass the yarn around the needle tip. The tension on the yarn is controlled by the yarn passing twice around the little finger.

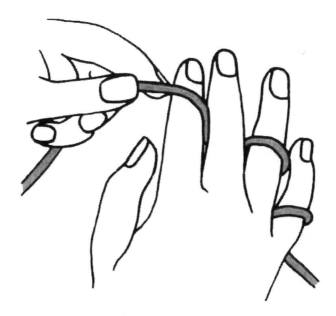

Fig. 15

Holding the Yarn - Method Two

Holding the yarn in your right hand, pass it under your little finger, over your third finger, under your center finger, and over your index finger. The index finger is used to pass the yarn around the needle tip. The tension here is created by gripping the yarn in the crook of your little finger.

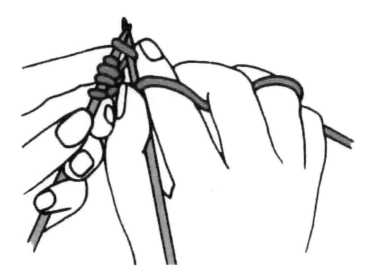

Fig. 16

Garter Stitch Knitting

When you knit every row the resulting pattern is called garter stitch. As you look at it, you will see that two rows of knitting produce one ridge. These ridges are very easy to count, but remember that each ridge equals two rows of knitting. Garter stitch is commonly used when knitting your first items. Below is what a garter stitch fabric looks like.

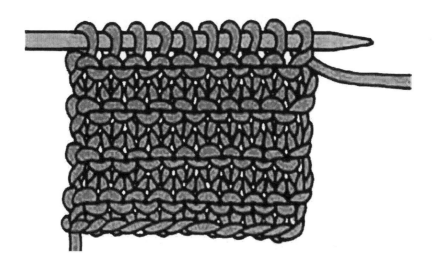

Fig. 17

To become comfortable with the knit stitch I would suggest that you take the time to knit at least 15 to 20 rows in the garter stitch fabric, knitting every row. Relax, enjoy the process, and don´t worry if your knitting is either a little loose or a little tight. This is because you are a beginner and you have not yet relaxed enough to produce a smooth fabric.

If you find that your knitting is very loose take extra care when wrapping the yarn around the right-hand needle to form a stitch and when pushing the old stitch off the left-hand needle. If your knitting is too tight, try not to tug or pull the yarn so tightly when forming your stitch.

Have you completed a small piece of knitting? Congratulations you have learned almost enough to complete your first proper garment, a scarf. All you need to know now is how to end your knitting — this is called casting off.

How to Cast Off

When you come to the end of your knitting, whether it is a simple square, a scarf or part of a larger project like the sleeve of a cardigan you need to close off the stitches so they won't unravel. Here's what to do:

1) Knit the first two stitches as you normally would.
2) Now, insert the left-hand needle into the **front** of the first stitch on the right-hand needle.
3) Pass the first stitch on the right-hand needle **over the second stitch** on the right-hand needle. One stitch has been bound off.

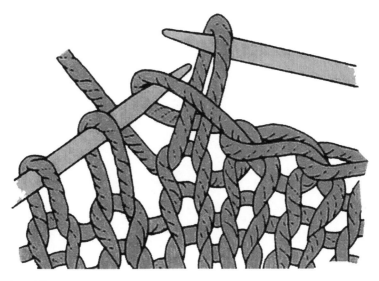

Fig. 18

4) To continue you simply knit the next stitch from the left needle as you normally would then repeat Steps 2 and 3 above until only one stitch remain on the right-hand needle.

5) Cut your yarn to about 4 inches in length. Remove the last stitch from the right-hand needle and draw the 4-inch tail through this stitch and pull it closed.

Because of the way the cast off row is formed, by pulling one stitch over the other, it can make this final row the tightest row of all your knitting. It can even be so tight as to distort your knitting by drawing it in too much. To prevent this from happening as a beginner, you can try casting off with a pair of needles one or two sizes larger than the ones you have been knitting with. Alternatively, you can simply try not to tug the yarn too tightly when forming your stitches. You want an even, smooth, relaxed last row.

You´re Ready to Begin You First Real Project

You have now acquired enough knitting skills to do your first project. I would suggest making a scarf, for yourself or a friend. A simple rectangular scarf will take approximately 300 to 400 yards of a medium weight yarn. Enjoy yourself, buy a yarn you really love, but in a light color. Check the label to be sure it is a medium #4 yarn. You will be using US size 5 needles.

Knitting a Scarf

Using the thumb method cast on 40 to 50 stitches. Knit all the stitches and all the rows creating a garter stitch fabric until you have reached the desired length, or until you have about 48 inches of yarn left. Cast off. Sew in any tails, and you´re done!

Perhaps a scarf was not your ideal first project. Well here´s the thing: to get really good at something you need practice, lots and lots of practice. A long scarf for yourself or a friend will give you exactly that, lots of stitches to knit, and time to improve so that soon you will be ready to move on to the purl stitch, the second most important stitch in knitting.

CHAPTER 4 - THE PURL STITCH

Once you know how to make the purl stitch, you can put it together with the knit stitch and create new fabrics. When you knit on one side of the fabric and purl on the other side the result is fabric that is smooth on the knit side and bumpy on the purl side. This is the fabric commonly seen on sweaters in shops and is known as stockinette stitch.

You can also combine the two stitches to make many different patterns. Below are examples of the knit side and purl side of a stockinette stitch fabric.

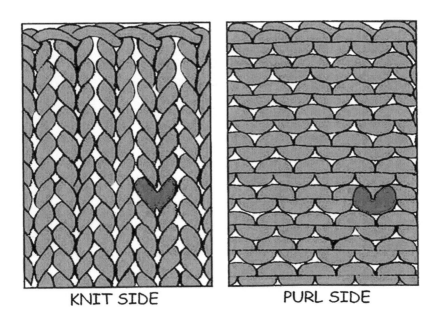

KNIT SIDE   PURL SIDE

Fig. 19

Before we learn the purl stitch, I am going to introduce you to another way of casting on. This method is known as the cable cast on. The cable cast on is less elastic than the thumb cast on and is very often used when knitting sweaters that is why I am introducing it here. As well, it is a little harder to drop a stitch off your needles when making the cable cast on or during the first row of knitting, this makes it ideal for beginners. Here's how you do it.

The Cable Cast On

First make a slip knot as you normally would, leaving a short tail and place the slip knot on your left-hand needle, pulling it up snugly, but not too tight.

Fig. 20

Knit into the slip knot, and bring the new loop you just created around to the right and slip it onto the left-hand needle. Do not slip the old loop of your left-hand

needle. You now have two stitches on your left-hand
needle.

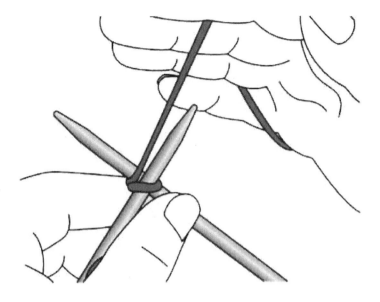

Fig. 21

Insert the right-hand needle between the two
stitches on your left-hand needle. Do not knit into the
stitches, place your needle between them.

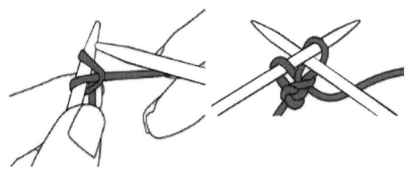

Fig. 22

Wrap the yarn around the right-hand needle, as
though you were going to knit and create a loop and bring
this loop through to the front.

Fig. 23

Bring the new loop around to the right and place it
on the left-hand needle. Continue inserting the right-hand

needle between the two stitches closest to the pointy end of your left-hand needle, then wrapping the yarn and bringing through a new loop and placing it on the left-hand needle until you have the number of cast on stitches you require.

Fig. 24

Making the Purl Stitch

1) With the yarn in front of the work, insert your right-hand needle from right to left through the front of the first stitch on the left-hand needle.

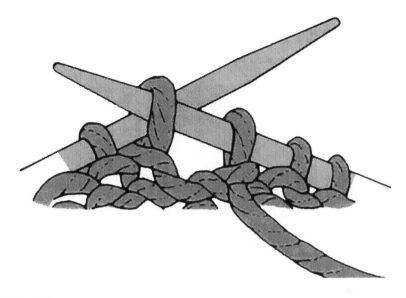

Fig. 25

2) Wind the yarn around the right-hand needle from right to left over the top of the needle.

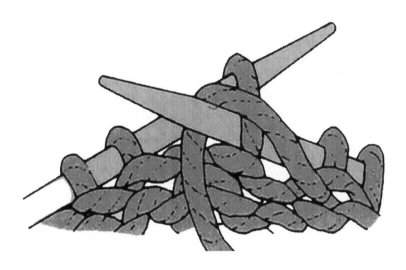

Fig. 26

3) Draw a loop through to the back.

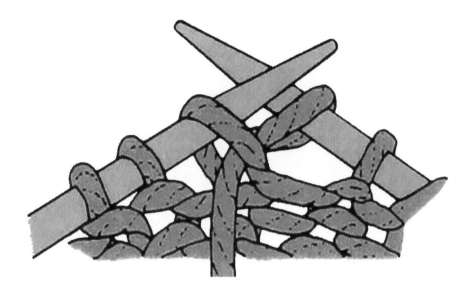

Fig.27

Slip the original stitch off the left-hand needle.

Fig. 28

Now that you have tried the purl stitch it might be a good time to cast on 30 stitches and knit about 30 rows of stockinette stitch. Simply cast on 30 stitches and then knit the first row. Once that row is completed, put the needle with the knitting in your left hand, take the yarn in your right hand and purl across row two. You have now completed 2 rows of stockinette stitch.

Continue knitting across the odd rows and purling across the even rows until you have completed 20 or 30 rows, forming a small square. When you reach a size, you are happy with cast off. You now have a sample of stockinette knitting to compare with your first square, which was knit in garter stitch. Can you see the differences? The garter stitch knitting is bumpy on both sides, and it lies flat and does not curl. The stockinette knitting has a smooth side and a bumpy side and its two edges curl in. This curl is one of the traits of stockinette stitch.

If you want to experiment with these two stitches I suggest you cast on 30 stitches using the cable cast on and then knit 5 rows and purl 1 row, knit 5 rows and purl 1 row, continue doing this until you have a small square and cast off. You can see how the knit and purl rows have created a textured pattern in your knitting.

These two simple stitches, knit and purl, plus a few ways of manipulating them, for example, knitting into the back instead of the front, or knitting two of them together, form the basis for the thousands upon thousands of knitting stitch patterns available to you.

CHAPTER 5 - INCREASING AND DECREASING

Without making increases or decreases in our knitting we would all end up wearing square or rectangular-shaped garments. Increases and decreases in the appropriate places allow you to shape your knitting as you go along, perhaps decreasing in the waist area and increasing for the chest or hips. In this chapter, I will show you a few of the most used increases and decreases.

Decreasing

When shaping a piece of knitting that is going to become a sweater, a knitter will often make two decreases, one on each side of the garment, so that the work is balanced. Some decreases naturally lean to the left and others to the right, so it is common to use a left-leaning decrease on the right side of a piece and a right-leaning decrease on the left edge, they both end up pointing towards the center, and they balance visually.

Right-leaning Decrease (Knit Two Together, or K2Tog)

In this case, your decrease will slant to the right. Therefore, if you have your knitting on your lap facing you,

you will generally apply this decrease somewhere towards the end of a knit row. When you are knitting following a pattern, you will find instructions perhaps something like this: Knit 10, SKP, Knit 30, K2Tog, Knit 10. What this is saying in plain English is Knit 10 stitches, then create a left-slanting decrease called a Slip, Knit, Pass (SKP), knit 30 stitches, then create a right-slanting decrease called Knit Two Together (K2Tog), knit 10 stitches. When you have completed your row you will have reduced it by 2 stitches and the total number will now be 48 instead of the 50 you began with.

To knit two stitches together, you simply insert your right-hand needle from front to back through the first and second on the left-hand needle. Place the point of your right-hand needle into the second stitch first and then the first stitch on the left-hand needle. Pass the working yarn around your right-hand needle to create a loop and pull the loop through both stitches to create a new stitch. Now slide the two stitches you have knit together off the left-hand needle.

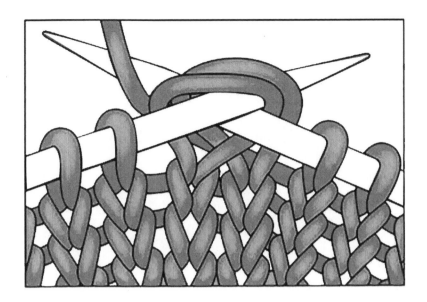

Fig. 29

Left-leaning Decrease (Slip, Knit, Pass or SKP)

To get your decrease to slant to the left you simply slip a stitch, knit the next stitch and then pass the slipped stitch over the knitted one. If you have your knitting on your lap facing you, you will generally apply this decrease somewhere just after the beginning of a knit row. In knitting patterns, this decrease is usually written as simply SKP.

Here is how it works. Insert your left-hand needle into the next stitch and do not knit it, simply slide it over to the right-hand needle as though you were going to knit it. You have just slipped one stitch.

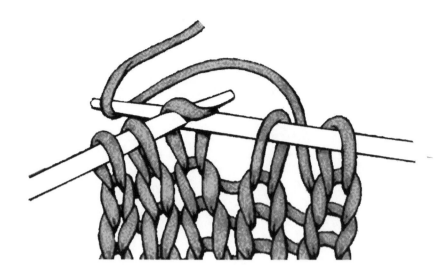

Fig. 30

Now, knit the next stitch on the left-hand needle and put the completed stitch on your right-hand needle. Using the tip of your left knitting needle, lift the slipped stitch over the knitted stitch, this decreases your number of stitches by one.

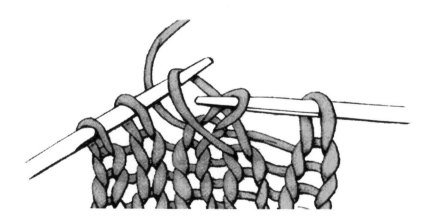

Fig. 31

If you take a little time to practice these two decreases, they will soon come naturally to you. I would suggest casting on about 30 stitches and knitting and purling in stockinette stitch for about 10 rows, this way you will be able to see the shape of your little square of knitting change as you incorporate the decreases.

Once you have completed 10 rows of knitting begin your decreases as follows:

1. Knit 3 stitches, SKP (slip, knit, pass slipped stitch over knitted stitch), knit to the last 5 stitches and then K2tog (knit 2 together).
2. Purl a row.
3. Knit a plain row.
4. Purl a row.
5. Knit 3 stitches, SKP, knit to the last 5 stitches, K2Tog, knit 3 stitches.
6. Purl a row.
7. Knit a plain row.
8. Purl a row.

Continue on repeating the 8 rows above until you have only 10 stitches left. Now, cast off the remaining stitches and keep this little piece of knitting as an example of matching decreases. Notice how the shape has changed?

Can you identify the slanted stitches on the left and right sides: one slanting left and one slanting right? You will often find these slanting stitches where knitted fabrics lean towards the left or right, for example, near the armholes on some sweaters.

Increasing

To increase you need to add, at the very least, one stitch to your knitting. Here I will show you two common methods to do just that. The first method leaves a visible mark on the front of your sweater, a tiny bump. The second method is much harder to detect with the naked eye. When your knitting pattern tells you to increase one stitch use the first method. When your knitting pattern tells you to "make one" use the second method.

Knit Into Back and Front

For this increase, you knit both the front and back loops of the next stitch on your needles. You will see this written as k1f,b, or k f/b, or even kfb, they all mean the same thing, "knit into the front and back of the next stitch."

Here is how you do it:

1) Insert your right needle into the next stitch on the left-hand needle and wrap the yarn around the right-hand needle creating a new stitch. Do not push the old stitch off your left-hand needle.

Fig. 32

2) Insert your right-hand needle again into the same stitch you just knitted, but this time put the point of your right-hand needle through the back of the stitch from right to left.

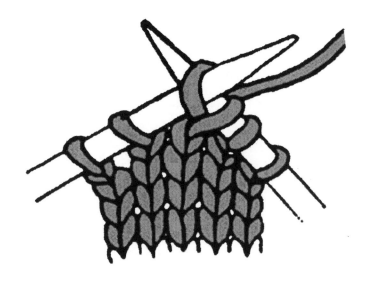

Fig. 33

Wrap the yarn around your right-hand needle. You now
have two stitches on your right-hand needle. You can slide
the old stitch off the left-hand needle.

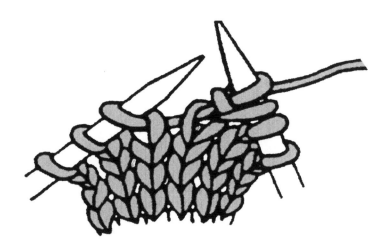

Fig. 34

Make One Increase

This increase draws up a loop from the row below, so you need to have knitted a few rows before you can try it. Go ahead and cast on a few stitches and then knit and purl 4 or 6 rows so that you have some knitting to work with. Here is how to do it:

1) Knit a few stitches. Now look down at the rows below. You can see the knitted stitches hanging there, held in place by the yarn connecting them to one another.

2) Look closely, and you will see little bars of yarn between the stitches. Choose the bar between the stitch you just knitted and the next stitch on your left-hand needle.

3) Pick up the bar between the stitches, from front to back and place it on your left-hand needle.

4) Use your right-hand needle to knit this bar through the back, this twists the bar into a stitch.

Fig. 35

5) The same stitch can also be worked on the purl side, just purl through the back of the bar for a purled "make one."

The Yarn Over Increase

The yarn over increase creates a stitch by wrapping the yarn around the right-hand needle. This creates a loop that does not really have a bottom, it is not attached to a stitch below it. So if you were to create a "yarn over" and then purl all the stitches, including the yarn over on the return pass, you will end up with a little hole in your work where the yarn over was worked. This is very useful in lace knitting.

You will find in many patterns that yarn overs are worked in pairs with knit 2 together. This is done to make little decorative holes in a pattern in your knitting. You might add a hole to your work by doing a yarn over, and then a few stitches later you will knit 2 together to remove a stitch, thus keeping the number of stitches in your work unchanged.

Here is how to knit a yarn over:

Knit a few stitches.

Now, wrap the working yarn over your right-hand needle from front to back. It will loosely drape over the needle.

Knit the next stitch.

Your yarn over is now held in place by knit stitches on either side of it.

Fig. 36

CHAPTER 6 - GETTING GAUGE

If you want to be a happy, contented knitter who knows that whatever you knit will fit the recipient, then this is the most important chapter of this little book. Gauge is what YOU, and ONLY YOU, create when knitting with a particular set of needles and a particular type of yarn. Let me explain further.

Let us say that both you and I buy the same yellow wool from the same yarn company. We both buy the same pair of size 6 needles and prepare to make the same baby sweater. We both cast on the correct number of stitches and knit for 20 rows. When we compare our knitting, mine is wider and taller than yours. How can this be? It could be that I knit more loosely than you do, or it could be that you are a tight knitter, pulling your stitches in carefully after every loop. It does not matter.

What matters is that on the pattern for the baby sweater it will state unequivocally that the gauge (sometimes patterns use the word "tension") should be X number of stitches and Y number of rows over 4 inches (or perhaps 20cm if it is a metric pattern.)

In order to make a baby sweater that will fit as described in the pattern, we have to match the exact number of stitches per inch. With rows, we can cheat a little bit. No one is going to complain if a sweater is an inch too long.

So how do we check our gauge? First, we take the yarn we will be using for our garment, and the needles recommended in the pattern, and we cast on enough stitches to measure approximately 6 inches. If you look at the label on your yarn, there will be a recommended number of stitches for 4 inches. For medium yarn, it is normally 14 to 18 stitches.

You will want to cast on a few extra stitches, say at least another 10, so you can measure your tension in the middle of your work and not from the edges. So, in this case, we would cast on 18 stitches, plus another 10 for a total of 28 stitches. Then we proceed to knit in whatever stitch the pattern uses, in our case as beginners we will probably be knitting in stockinette stitch. So we will knit and purl our 28 stitches until our work has reached approximately 6 inches, then we will cast off.

Now we have a gauge swatch which we can measure to see if we are getting gauge. Here´s how to do it.

Lay your gauge swatch down on a flat surface. If the edges are curling in too much, very gently pin them down **without stretching your knitting.**

Place a straight pin beside a knitted stitch about 1 inch in from the edge of your knitting.

Take a measuring tape, or a ruler, and measure across the row exactly 4 inches and place another straight pin next to the nearest stitch.

Now, carefully count the number of stitches between the two straight pins. If you have the number suggested in the pattern you are good to go. You can cast on and knit your project.

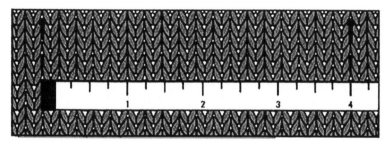

Fig. 37

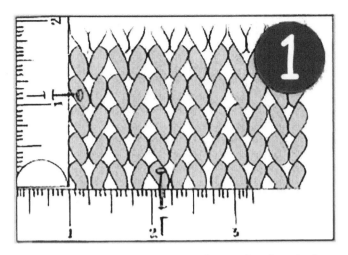

Fig. 38 – this illustration shows both stitches and rows being counted

However, if you have fewer or more stitches between the two pins you will need to change your needles and try again. Why?

Let us assume that you are out by two stitches over 4 inches. That is half a stitch per inch in the width of your knitting. If you are knitting a cardigan for an adult male the instructions might be as follows:

Cast on 160 stitches at a tension of 4 stitches to the inch.

160 stitches divided by 4 stitches per inch = 40 inches, the average chest size

160 stitches divided by 4.5 stitches per inch = 35 inches, *much too small*

I did not "get gauge" on the first sweater I knit for myself, which was a boat neck pullover. I just choose a pair of knitting needles I liked and some yarn I liked and cast on. I did not understand what gauge or tension was. When it was completed the sweater was so large I gave it to my brother, who is over six feet tall!

So, if you are getting more stitches in your gauge swatch than is indicated in the pattern, you need to switch to a larger needle. Try the next size thicker needle. If you were using a 5, try a 6.

If you are getting fewer stitches in your gauge swatch than is indicated in the pattern, you will need to switch to a smaller needle. If you were using a 5, try a 4.

Then, redo your gauge swatch. That's right, redo it. You need to be sure that you are matching the gauge required otherwise you will knit something that may not fit.

Some people hate swatching, they find it boring. I would much rather have a sweater that fits than worry about being bored. I often work on my knitted gauge swatches while watching television or listening to music. The rows seem to go quickly, and it is soon done. I save the swatch as well. Sometimes you end up with very little yarn left over once you have completed your knitting and you can always unravel the gauge swatch and use that yarn to sew up your finished garment.

There are gauge measuring tools available to purchase, they are usually a metal rectangle with an area cut out. You lay them over your knitted swatch and count the number of stitches and rows that appear in the cutout area.

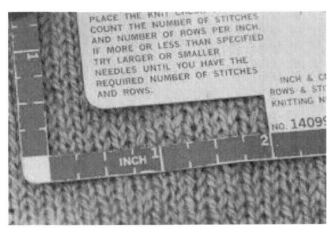

Fig. 39

CHAPTER 7 - DEALING WITH PROBLEMS AND MISTAKES

We all make mistakes, it's how we learn. For most of us making a mistake isn't the issue, it is knowing how to fix it. Here is where I will show you how to fix the most common problems novice knitters run into.

Correct Orientation of your Knitting

You were interrupted in the middle of a row and put your knitting down. Hours, even days later, you come back to it but cannot remember which is the front and which is the back. Remember this: when you are knitting, the working yarn should always be on the right-hand side, and it should be trailing down behind your needles.

Look at your work. If the working yarn is facing you, then you are looking at the back of your work. If the working yarn is on the left-hand needle, then you are looking at the back of your work. Simply turn it over so that the working yarn is trailing down the back and the needle that holds it is in your right hand.

Correct Orientation of the Knit Stitch.

Stitches can become twisted if you do not realize how a stitch should be oriented on the needle. Take a look at your knitting after you have knit a few stitches into a row. Now, look at the next stitch waiting on the left-hand needle to be knit. You will see that it is an upside-down U shape, hanging over the left needle. If it is oriented correctly, you will notice that the stitch hanging on the needle is slightly slanted, the back of the stitch will be slanted slighted to the left.

The side of the stitch closest to you should be closer to the tip of the needle than the side of the stitch farthest away from you. See the illustrations below. Why is this important? If your stitch is sitting the wrong way on the needle and you knit into as you normally would, you will end up with a visible twisted stitch in your knitting.

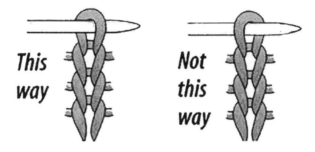

Fig. 40

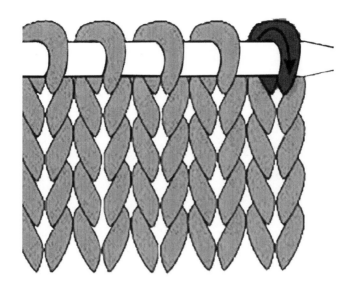

Fig. 41

If a Thumb Cast On Stitch Drops Off During the First Row

This is a common problem when first learning to knit because the thumb cast on is simply a series of loops and they are not yet anchored properly. As you knit the first row one of the stitches will drop off leaving you with a section of slack yarn hanging down. To fix this, you need to twist it back into an e shape.

First, put the **right-hand needle** under the slack from **back to front**. Then put the **left-hand needle** through this slack yarn on the right-hand needle **from the**

front towards the back. (See illustration.) Finally, wrap the yarn around the right-hand needle as you normally would to knit and knit as usual.

Fig. 42

A Stitch Has Slipped Off the Needle

No worries at all, this happens all the time, especially if your yarn is slippery. If the stitch is still intact, you can see the loop, and it has not come undone, you can simply rehang it on the left-hand needle.

However, be sure to see the section above entitled "Correct Orientation of the Knit Stitch" to remind you which way the stitch should hang on the left needle.

You Have Dropped a Stitch and it has Unravelled

This is a common knitting error. It happens to all of us sooner or later. You accidentally drop a stitch while knitting but do not notice. A few rows later, due to the twisting of the yarn, while you are knitting, the stitch slowly unravels creating a small ladder in your knitting.

The easiest way to fix this is to use a medium-sized crochet hook to help you rehang the undone stitches. See the illustrations below.

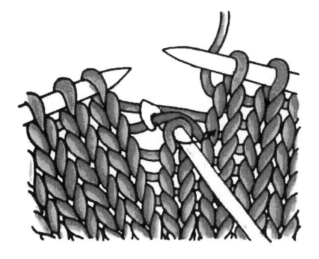

Fig. 43

As you can see in the illustration, you take your crochet hook and put it through the first loop you come to in the ladder where you stitch has dropped down. You snag the draped yarn with a crochet hook, as illustrated and pull it through that loop.

Continue in this way until you have rehung all the rows that have dropped and place the completed stitch on the left-hand needle to be knitted.

Be sure to make sure the stitch is positioned correctly (see stitch orientation above) and carry on knitting.

You have Dropped a Stitch Along the Edge

Dropping a stitch along the edge is common with beginners, and you often do not notice it for a few rows. This is why it is good practice to count the number of stitches on your needles every few rows. If there are less than there should be you can stop knitting and look for that dropped stitch.

To repair a dropped edge stitch, you will use the medium sized crochet hook again, hooking the stitch up along the edge. See the illustrations below.

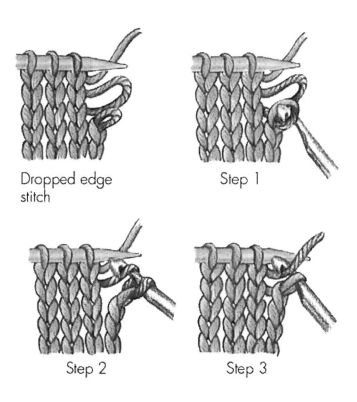

Dropped edge stitch

Step 1

Step 2

Step 3

Fig. 44

If You Need to go Back in the Current Row

If you have made a mistake, twisted a stitch or see a dropped stitch in your current row of knitting, you will have to go back. The easiest way to do this is to unknit your stitches until you reach the stitch you need to fix. In knitter's slang, this is called "tinking", tink is merely knit spelled backward. Look at the illustrations below. As you can see you are removing the knitted stitches and placing

the stitches from the row below back onto your left-hand
needle one by one.

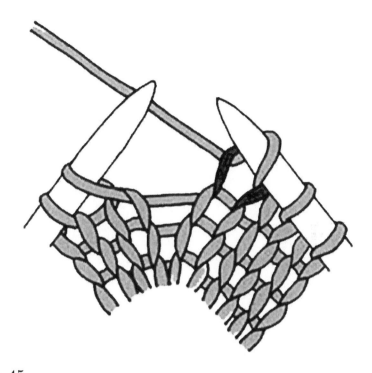

Fig. 45

To take out stitches, you have just knit you take your left-
hand needle and place it into the **stitch below the first
stitch on your right-hand needle**. The dark stitch in
illustration 45.

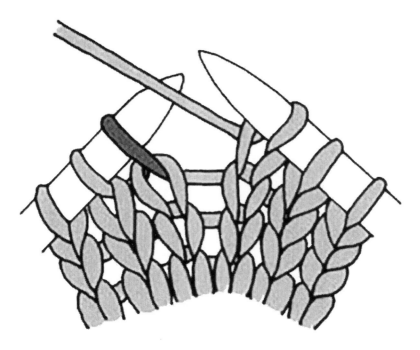

Fig. 46

Then slide the right-hand needle out of the old stitch. One stitch now returned to the left needle. The dark stitch in illustration 46. Repeat this process with the next stitch until you have removed the knitted stitches and arrive at the stitch where your mistake has occurred.

If You Need To Go Back Many Rows

Sometimes you won't notice a mistake until many rows later. You lay the knitting down and suddenly see you have twisted a stitch and it is really going to show. What to do? Well, most knitters unravel their work back to one row below the row with the error and then knit those rows again.

The first thing to do is to count how many rows you have to rip out and write that down somewhere as an *aide memoire* because you will have to go back in your pattern instructions exactly that many rows. Mark this row with a piece of contrasting yarn or a safety pin. Then in order not to lose any stitches, the easiest way to go back is to slip all the stitches off your right-hand needle. Yikes!

Now, take your right-hand needle and insert it through the front of every knit stitch in the row you have marked. See the illustration below.

Fig. 47

As you can see in illustration 47, the **right-hand needle is entering the first leg of the knit stitch from the back, from right to left.** Once you have picked up all of the stitches across the row, set the needle down and pick up the working yarn at the top of your knitting and carefully, gently pull it back, unravelling the rows of knitting.

It will stop unravelling at the row where you have inserted your right-hand needle.

Fig. 48

If Your Knitting Has a Hole In It

Sometimes we get to the end of a piece of knitting without realizing we have made a mistake. You dropped a stitch and didn't notice it. You have two choices here.

1) Rip the knitting back to the row below where you dropped the stitch and reknit.

2) Find the dropped stitch and secure it by threading an 8-inch piece of matching yarn through it. Sew the tails of this yarn to the wrong side of your knitting. If you are careful, the result may not show on the right side of your knitting.

CHAPTER 8 - PUTTING YOUR WORK TOGETHER

You have finally completed all the pieces of knitting to make a sweater but how do you actually put it together? If you are sewing garter stitch pieces together follow this method. (See illustrations 49 and 50 below.)

1) Place the two pieces to be joined face up on a flat surface.

2) Take a tapestry needle under one of the garter ridges, close to the edge of the piece.

3) Go across to the second piece and take your tapestry needle under the matching ridge.

4) Go back to the first piece and take your tapestry needle under the next ridge. Repeat steps 2 and 3 several times and then holding the bottom edge firmly, gently pull the stitches taut.

Fig. 49

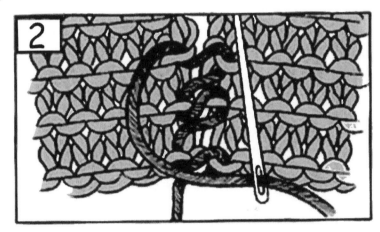

Fig. 50

Mattress Stitch

Mattress Stitch is commonly used to join stockinette fabric together. When done correctly it is a virtually invisible seam. To join rows to rows, e.g., the side seams of a sweater:

1) Place the two pieces to be joined face up on a flat surface.

2) Take a tapestry needle under the cast on the edge of the first piece.

3) Put the tapestry needle under the cast on the edge of the second piece.

4) Return to the first piece and to the space your yarn came out of. Take the needle down, from front to back, between the edge stitch and the next stitch and then bring the needle up again one row later.

5) Return to the second piece and to the space your yarn came out of. Take the needle down, from front to back between the edge stitch and the next stitch. Bring the needle up two rows later.

6) Return to the first piece, and to the space your yarn came out of. Take the needle down, from front to back between the edge stitch and the next stitch and come up two rows later.

7) Repeat steps 5 and 6, alternating between the left and right pieces of your knitting.

8) When you have completed 5 to 7 rows, hold the bottom of your pieces with your left thumb and forefinger and with your right hand pull the stitches taut.

9) Continue in this fashion until you come to the end of the seam. At the end of the seam close your seam by taking the needle into the final bound off stitch on the right-hand side and then under the first bound off stitch of the piece on the left-hand side.

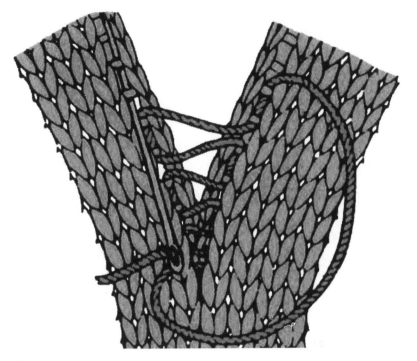

Fig. 51

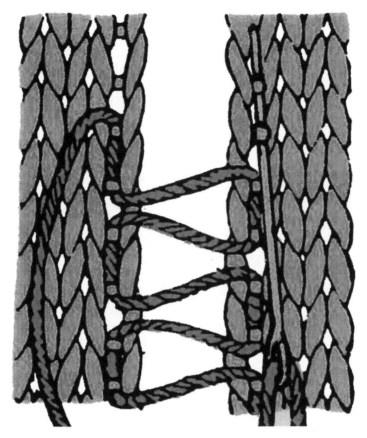

Fig. 52

Mattress Stitch to Join Stitch to Stitch

When joining stitches to stitches, as in a shoulder seam, you work the mattress stitch under one complete stitch. (See illustration below.) The cast off row is turned under, and you end up with a nearly invisible seam.

Fig 53

With the right sides facing you, align the shoulders and insert the yarn needle under one complete stitch as shown. Work inside the bind-off edge for a seamless look.

APPENDIX

Every knitting pattern you purchase specifies a particular weight of yarn. Some even specify particular brands of yarn. Below is a yarn chart to help you substitute yarns in case you are unable to find a particular yarn specified in a pattern.

Substituted yarn will be slightly different from that specified in the pattern making it especially important to complete a gauge swatch to ensure you are knitting to the required gauge or tension.

	1 SUPER FINE	2 FINE	3 LIGHT	4 MEDIUM	5 BULKY	6 SUPER BULK
Yarn Weight						
Also Called	Sock Fingering Baby	Sport Baby	DK Light Worsted	Worsted Afghan	Chunky Craft Aran	Bulky Roving Rug
Knit Gauge Range in	27 to 32 sts	23 to 26 sts	21 to 24 sts	16 to 20 sts	12 to 15 sts	6 to 11 sts

Stockinette to 4 inches						
Recommended Needle US	1 to 3	3 to 5	5 to 7	7 to 9	9 to 11	13 to 19
Recommended Needle Metric	2mm to 3.25 mm	3.25 mm to 3.75 mm	3.75 mm to 4.50 mm	4.5 mm to 5.5 mm	5.5 mm to 8 mm	9 mm to 16 mm

COMMON ABBREVIATIONS FOUND IN KNITTING PATTERNS

BO	bind off
CO	cast on
CM	centimeter (2.5 cm to 1 inch)
DPS(S)	double pointed needles
K	Knit
K2TOG	knit two stitches together
KB	knit into the back of the stitch
KF	knit into the front of the stitch
KF&B	knit into the front and back of the stitch
K-WISE	knit-wise, as if to knit
M1	make one (see increases)
M	meter equals 100 cm.
P	Purl
P2TOG	Purl 2 together
P-WISE	purl-wise, as if to purl
RS	right side of work
RSS	reverse stockinette stitch – the bumpy or purl side of the fabric will be the right side of your finished garment

SL	slip – transfer one stitch from the left to right-hand needle without knitting it
SKP	slip 1, knit 1, pass slipped stitch over knitted stitch
ST(S)	stitch or stitches
YB	yarn in back of the work
YF	with yarn in front of the work
WS	wrong side of the garment, the non-public side
YO	Yarn over – a stitch produced by laying or wrapping the yarn over the right-hand needle.

Printed in Great Britain
by Amazon